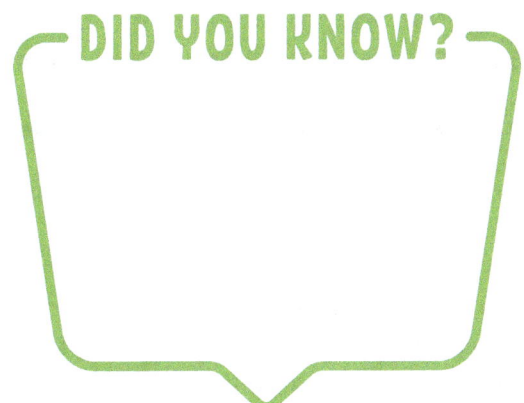

THE STORIES OF

GREENSHIRE

AMREEN FATIMA

FanatiXx Publication

AM/56, Basanti Colony, Rourkela 769012, Odisha
ISO 9001: 2015 CERTIFIED

Website: www.fanatixxpublication.com

© Copyright 2020, Amreen Fatima

All rights reserved. No part of this book may be reproduced, stored in a retrieval system, or transmitted, in any form by any means, electronic, mechanical, magnetic, optical, chemical, manual, photocopying, recording or otherwise, without prior written consent of the author.

"Stories of Greenshire"

By: Amreen Fatima

ISBN: 978-93-5605-163-8

1st Edition.

Cover Designer: Sagar Chand Samal
Illustrator: Amreen Fatima

Price: INR 499/-

Printed and Typeset by: BooksClub.in

The opinions/ contents expressed in this book are solely of the author and do not represent the opinion/ stands/ thoughts of FanatiXx.

ACKNOWLEDGEMENT

This book is dedicated to my older son Aameen Ali who seldom reads story books, and to my younger son Ayzel Ali who is still too young to read anything.

I would also like to thank my parents (Mr. Liyaquat Hussain and Mrs. Ajab Sadriwala) and sister (Siddiqua Fatima), who have always inspired me, and my backbone, my ever - supporting husband (Sarfraz Nawaz).

DID I GET THE BEST?

Mrs. and Mr. Kindle lived in a beautiful house surrounded by a jungle with many friendly animals and birds.

They had a little boy named 'Thrilly.' Turkey was their pet, who was also his best friend. Turkey and Thrilly used to call themselves T - Buddies and this 'T' stood for both starting letters of their name and their fondness for 'Tea' which they used to drink together, gossiping about all other beings, including humans and animals.
One day, while talking about random topics, they started arguing about each other's looks.

DID YOU KNOW?

Turkey Birds-
1. They can change the colors of their head.
2. Their poop can determine whether they are male or female.
3. They sleep in trees at night.

Turkey said to Thrilly that he was just a primary human with no particular functioning body parts, unlike 'Aley,' who was giant with a beautiful trunk and big ears and could crush anything he stamped on, or like 'Croco,' who had thick skin with a big mouth and could eat almost anything. She further explained to Thrilly how she was gossiping of Croco a lot as one day, he was about to engulf her too in one bite like he engulfed her aunt Turkey and her three daughters. Thrilly got scared by learning how mighty 'The Croco' and 'The Aley' were. He also started feeling that he was a primary human being with no particular body part to be called mighty or even to call beautiful, as he didn't even have beautiful eyes like those of Owly's.

These thoughts made Thrilly gloomy, and he started living a sad life. He kept thinking about whether he looked basic and had no unique body part that could make him different from others.

One day, he went to his mother, asking her if she had given birth to a boy with no unique body parts like Aley's or Croco's.

He cried and yelled at his mother that it was her fault that he looked the way he did and that she was not a good mother.

This whole incident was making Mrs. Kindle tense. But she was clueless about convincing her boy that he looked the best the way he was. Mr. Kindle overheard the conversation between Mrs. Kindle and Thrilly.

So later that day, Mr. Kindle asked Thrilly, "Do you know my boy, when you were in your mother's womb, I had to toil a lot for how you look now?"

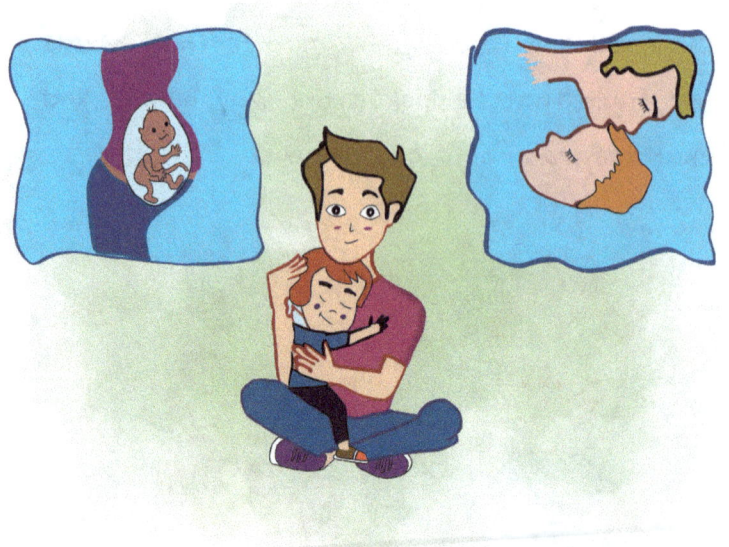

Thrilly got triggered as he was already very upset about his looks and quickly inquired of his father, "What did you do, PEPE?"

Mr. Kindle continued, "Before a baby is born, the baby's father is called by God to choose whatever is the best for his child. And so, I was also called by God to select the best for you." Thrilly said, "So exciting, PEPE! It's so exciting! Tell me more, PEPE. Did you get the best for me?"

"Hold your horses, Thrilly," smiled Mr. Kindle. Thrilly reluctantly answered, "But PEPE, I don't have horses."

"HAHAHAHA! No at all a problem, Thrilly." Laughed Mr. Kindle and made Thrilly sit on his lap. He then narrated, "There was a lot of rush, so many babies to be born. Parents were tripping over each other."

Thrilly interrupted, "What was it about? Did you get the best for me?"

Mr. Kindle cuddled him and planted a kiss on his forehead, "My love, No one is born best but becomes the best by good work and great thought."

This was too difficult for Thrilly to understand, so he ignored it. He started fidgeting.

"Tell me! Tell me, PEPE! Did you get the best for me?" Thrilly inquired restlessly.

Mr. Kindle nodded and replied, "I want you to decide – Did I get the best for you?"

Thrilly felt like a grown-up and replied responsibly, "Okies, so, tell me, PEPE. What exactly were the choices?"

Mr. Kindle continued, "It was a long queue there. Everybody wanted the best."

"Long queue for what PEPE?" asked Thrilly.

"Long queue to get your NOSE, my love." Answered Mr. Kindle.

Thrilly quickly touched his NOSE and started wondering, "Long queue for this nose PEPE."

"YES, Thrilly! This tiny nose of yours." He continued, "It was a huge place, with many people, all gathered to get the best nose for their wards.

It took me days to get my chance, and finally, I reached the BIG TABLE.

And... on that big table were displayed different noses.

All of the different kinds."

"What were the different types of noses displayed? And PEPE! Did you get the best for me?" Thrilly interrupted. Mr. Kindle continued, "There was a big Nose just as big as your hand. Like the one an Elephant has that works as an 'All-Purpose Tool.' Multifunctional! An elephant's trunk can be used for bathing, holding a branch to swat flies, making tools, and even comforting its young ones. Then, there was a 6-inch-long nose, just like the one proboscis's monkey that helps him make friends by producing a loud sound. There was a Foraging Tool-type nose, just like your friend in the neighborhood, Aardvark has.

There was a nose that could be used as a navigation aid, just like the one Star-Nosed mole has. And so many more ...."

Thrilly was convinced that it had been a difficult job to select one. So, he quickly asked, "Weren't you confused, PEPE?"

Mr. Kindle took a deep breath and said, "Well! Not really, Thrilly, because there was a Helping Angel helping everyone to shortlist two options out of many given choices. He helped me too. So, I took two noses, a cute one, this one, he pointed at Thrilly's nose, and the other a big one – the one I told you about, the multifunctional, the – purpose tool." Thrilly shouted, "I know that one, which Aley has but PEPE! Did you get the best for me?" "Umm, Well! You are the one to decide whether I got the best for you or not?" Replied Mr. Kindle.

DID YOU KNOW?

Elephant - the largest land animal
1. Elephant trunk has 150,000 muscles.

2. Their trunk can suck up to 8 liters of water, and they use their trunk as a snorkel when swimming.

3. Elephant tusks are enlarged incisor teeth that continue growing throughout their lives.

Thrilly quickly closed his eyes and imagined himself with a trunk, just like Aley's. He felt himself to be mighty. Imagining himself carrying heavy logs in his long trunk, sprinkling water on Turkey, and making a thundering sound by stamping his feet on the ground. He enjoyed it a lot, having thought he had a trunk. But then something tickled in his nose, his eyes opened, and he sneezed loudly. Mr. Kindle quickly helped, cleaned his nose, and pleaded to be careful. Thrilly consoled his father that he knew very well that he was allergic to pollen grains and that his father should not worry about him. Thrilly once again closed his eyes and imagined himself sneezing with his trunk. It was disgusting! All the walls around him were filled with gluey discharge from his big snake-like nose.

It was a mess each time he sneezed. He felt embarrassed, and eventually, his friends avoided and mocked him. Especially Turkey, who teased him by calling him 'Gunky Thrilly.'

"I am not a Gunky Thrilly! Please Don't call me Gunky!" shouted Thrilly and opened his eyes.
"What happened, Thrilly? Who is calling you Gunky? Are you Okay?" inquired Mr. Kindle.

"Yes! Yes, PEPE, I am excellent, and I think you have made a correct choice bringing this (Thrilly points his nose) for me. This has never made me feel embarrassed in front of anyone and above all, I can even smell the sweet perfume you are wearing. I actually a... kind of Love my nose." Explained Thrilly.
Mr. Kindle felt relieved. "So, I got the best Nose for you, and there was a long queue...."
"Long Queue again, PEPE????" questioned Thrilly.

"Yes! Yes!! My Love a longer queue than before. I had to wait for weeks to have my turn come." Mr. Kindle answered.

"Really, PEPE!! About what was the long queue PEPE?"

Mr. Kindle continued, "It was a long queue, and exactly after two weeks, two days, and two hours of waiting, it was my turn to choose Eyes for you.

It was a huge place, and from where I didn't... I didn't understand exactly where the pairs of eyes dangling on thread coming from. But all the other parents over there murmured that they were coming directly from heaven.

All different types of eyes. Different colors – Black, brown, blue, green, hazel, and so many more. Different in size – tiny, small, big, and very big."

"Did Helping Angel come?" asked Thrilly.
"Yes! Yes, my Love, this time it was Eye Fairy who helped me shortlist two pairs of eyes for you. One pair of eyes was the one you have, small but pretty." Mr. Kindle replied. Thrilly blinked his eyes to flatter and asked, "What about the other pair, and did you get the best for me, PEPE?"
"The other pair was that of Owly's. You decide, Thrilly, whether I get the best pair of Eyes or not?"

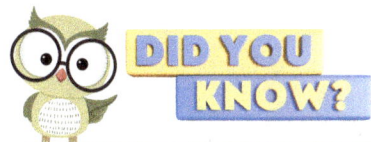

DID YOU KNOW?

1. A group of owls is called a parliament.
2. Owls can turn their heads as far as 270 degrees.
3. The smallest owl in the world is the Elf Owl. They are between 12 cm and 15 cm tall.

Thrilly found it fascinating. He quickly closed his eyes and imagined himself with those of Owl. Big and beautiful. He imagined his friends loved his eyes and everyone admired his eyes. He was way too happy imagining himself with an owl's eyes even. Turkey was even envious of his beautiful eyes, but then he remembered that Owly was nocturnal and could even see at night.

Next, he imagined seeing all the

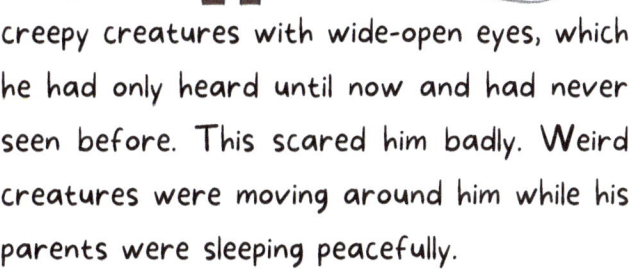

creepy creatures with wide-open eyes, which he had only heard until now and had never seen before. This scared him badly. Weird creatures were moving around him while his parents were sleeping peacefully.

"What a nightmare!", Thrilly screamed and opened his eyes. He hugged his father tight and told him he had chosen the best pair of eyes for him.

But Mr. Kindle continued, "It was a long Queue; parents were tripping over each other, and this time they did so for your mouth."

Thrilly got excited all over again. Deciding whether his father had made a correct choice or not had become a game for him, and he was enjoying it. He asked, "You even had the choice for my mouth. Just tell me the PEPE choices so I can decide if you got the best for me?" "Of course, my Love. There was a long queue, and everybody wanted the best. God gave me two choices. There were two mouths kept in a big chest. On that chest was written 'Get the Best for your Love - Mr. Kindle.' One mouth was huge and ferocious with so many teeth in it. All of them were so sharp. They could chew almost everything and anything, just like that Croco could do. The other was one that you have. So, tell me, Thrilly, Did I get the best for you?" asked Mr. Kindle.

1. Crocodiles are reptiles.
2. Crocodiles have the strongest bite of any animal in the world.
3. Some crocodile species can weigh over 1200 kg.

As Thrilly was already enjoying the game of judging his father's choice. He quickly closed his eyes and started imagining himself with a crocodile's mouth. It looked ferocious and robust. He felt as mighty as the other animals Turkey used to tell him about. But then he remembered that Turkey also said Croco is fond of 'Turkeys.'

Next, he imagined that his best friend, Turkey, was no longer his friend, and he felt lonely with no friends. He felt even sadder than before. He opened his eyes and started crying. He had probably understood that he was wrong, and his father had always made the best choice for him. "You made all correct choices for me. My Nose, My Eyes, and My Mouth...everything".

Mr. Kindle caressed him and said, "Yes! Everybody is best in their way. My Love, whatever we have, our nose, our eyes, our mouth, everything is apt according to our needs, but we can make them best by using them correctly.

We must love ourselves the way we are. Great work and thoughts are the keys to becoming mighty and great."

Thrilly got a lesson and once again started living a happy life.

Fluffy of Greenshire

Zinker, Zonky, Fluffy, and Mala belong to Honky pack of the Greenshire jungle. Their pack has some strict rules engraved on a Banyan tree bark using the sharp nails of their ancestors; the very first rule was,

"Whether its day or night,
Or the Earth turns upside,
Honkies will never step outside."

These rules were not only engraved on the tree bark but on every Honky's heart too. Not a single Honky dared to step outside the jungle. But mother nature had its plan, and this time she had chosen Fluffy for that. Fluffy was the cutest and bravest among all. He was born a singer; his voice can mesmerize anyone, but Fluffy had a weird weakness of chasing butterflies.

If he sees a butterfly, he can't resist following it. He would never harm it but wanted to chase it.

The colorful butterfly wings inspire him to sing and live life vibrantly.

1. They can learn over 100 words and gestures.
2. Dog noses are at least 40x more sensitive than ours!
3. They only sweat from their paws and must cool down by panting.

Did you know..

It was 21st April 2022 when Fluffy was chasing one butterfly and accidentally stepped outside the Greenshire, and when he realized what he had done, it was already too late. The night was howling loud, and stars were twinkling far above. Not a single tree he knew, and even the butterfly had mysteriously disappeared. The only thing he could see now was a big black slide-like thing and some dangerous monsters rolling on it. Monsters had two bright suns on their face and made some Brum Brum noise. Some of them also made some BEEP! BEEP sound. Few monsters were massive, and others were comparatively smaller in size. Monsters blow out some black and suffocating substance from a hole in their backside. Fluffy figured out it to be a monster's Fart.

Monster's Fart had some dangerous chemicals that made Fluffy tired and sick. This Monster's Fart was too suffocating even to breathe; it had changed the color of Fluffy's fur. His fur was no whiter in color but had turned brown. Monsters look tough and carry humans on them. Fluffy had heard about Humans in Greenshire. His parents had once warned him about Humans. Humans are the most dangerous creatures in the world. They were in huge numbers and had the power to do anything. Fluffy was the bravest among his pack today, but he felt scared and lonely.

He then remembered Rule Two of Greenshire, which says:

"Whether the problem is big or small
Or the Earth seems to be rock and roll,
Honkies sing loudly to call."

So, to call his pack, he started singing. His voice was so mesmerizing that all the monsters stopped on the black slide, and all humans gathered around him. When Fluffy stopped singing, he got heebity – jeebities seeing humans around him. He had no clue what to do next. He just crouched his body and sat there gloomily.

By that time, Fluffy had understood clearly, that he was in grave danger, and above all, he was too hungry and exhausted.

He then recalls Rule number three, which says,

"Whether the day is worst or perfect
Or does the Earth feel unfortunate,
Honkies eat whatever they get."

So, when he saw a piece of the loaf in one human child's hand, he just snatched it and ate it. Fluffy didn't want to do so, but he was abiding by the rules.

Instead of screaming at Fluffy, the human child smiled back, which was very unusual for Fluffy because Fluffy has known Humans only as bad rather worst creatures of the world.

A couple of minutes later, another giant Monster came with a red light blinking on his back. That monster stopped next to Fluffy, and a bulky human came out of it who tightly held Fluffy and made him sit on that giant Monster. Fluffy was scared near death. He kept on singing loudly to call his pack but all in vain. After some time, Fluffy closed his eyes and pretended to sleep on the Monster when he heard that Bulky human, who forcefully made Fluffy sit on that giant Monster talking to himself and pressing the buttons on it. He said, "Alpha I Coming! Alpha I Coming!

Mission accomplished ! I have rescued the pup, standing in the middle of the C - Block highway, Redshire Road which was causing a traffic jam, and now everything is sorted." The Monster replied, "Great Job! Now bring the dog to StrEEEEEeeeeee... eeeee ...eeee..." It was a disturbing and screeching sound that Big Monster was making, and then Fluffy heard Bulky human banging his heavy hand on the Monster and saying, "Not Again! You crazy transistor! It has stopped working again; now, what should I do?" Fluffy had no idea what on Earth was happening. He just wished it to be a horrifying nightmare.

Fluffy was mentally exhausted, so he fell asleep on the giant Monster in no time. When he opened his -eyes, he found himself chained to a pole. It seemed an annoying place for Fluffy, full of humans and human things; he could barely see any trees, shrubs, or herbs he was familiar with.

He was missing Zinker, Zonky, Mala, his parents, and everybody in Greenshire. He felt pathetic and unfortunate and wanted to go back to Greenshire.

To get himself free, he pushed hard against the pole to which he was chained.

Now, he had lost all his patience and started crying loud. The unfortunate horrible night had passed. It was **22**nd April **2022** now.

While Fluffy was crying, another human gave him something to eat and water to drink. The food humans gave them was pretty different from what he ate but tasty. After having food, Fluffy felt a little better, but he was still gloomy until he heard a mouse quickening from nowhere. "Are you lost, my dear?" Inquired the

old dirty mouse. Fluffy looked everywhere to find out where precisely the voice was coming from. "Here! Here, my boy, I am right next to your paw." Mouse said. He added, "You can call me Grand Mousy; I live here (he pointed to a hole next to the pole to which Fluffy was chained)." Fluffy finally got someone to talk with other than the human he hates. He quickly replied, "Yes, Grandy, I am lost. I was chasing a yellow butterfly and stepped outside the Greenshire."

Mouse – Plural is Mice
1. Female mice can start giving birth when they are just two months old.
2. Mice eat between 15 and 20 times a day.
3. A female mouse can birth 150 mice in a year.

"Greenshire! Did you say Greenshire!" Grandy interrupted.

"Yes! Yes! I said Greenshire." Fluffy got excited that maybe Grandy could help him return to Greenshire. But Grandy, on the other hand, had different views about Greenshire. Grandy replied quickly, "I hate Greenshire and especially the Honkies of Greenshire, who think themselves to be the best and most civilized creatures."

Fluffy's hopes drowned, and he was left with nothing to speak, but he still dared to ask without revealing that he was a Honky, "What made you so upset? Why do you hate Greenshire and specially Honkies?"

Grandy replied, "It's a long story. Moreover, it is all over now. I don't like lingering on to past."

"You, my young boy, you tell me about yourself." He further added. Fluffy was gloomy, but now he wanted to know why

Grandy hated his grandfather that much. He also felt that since Grandy knows his grandfather, he must know the way back to Greenshire.

This made him recall yet another rule of Greenshire,

> "Whether the situation is tough or simple or the Earth seems to be terrible, Honkies never give up on any riddle."

The reason behind Grandy's hatred was probably a riddle for a young puppy who was lost but was loyal to his clan and was still abiding by its rule. To tell the reason behind Grandy's hatred for Honkies Fluffy said, "You know, Grandy! I am feeling lonely and scared. Whenever I felt so, back in Greenshire, my mother told me stories and distracted me. I am missing her terribly. I wish she would be here to help me", and he started whining. Grandy was an old rat with a kind heart; he felt emotional looking at young Fluffy and replied, "Please stop crying, my boy. You are young and brave. I can't replace your mother, but I can tell a story to distract you and just for information.

information. I am an excellent storyteller." Fluffy's plan works out. He quickly stopped crying and added, "I hope Grandy, you won't mind telling me that long story, the one that made you hate Honky."

Grandy understood that this young puppy was stubborn but he had started adoring him for no reason. So, he took a deep breath and narrated. "Years back, when I was young. The leader of Honky clan and I were close friends. We lived together like a family in Greenshire. There was an old Banyan tree, very dear to me; I had written rules for Honkies on that because, as you know, it's very easy for us rats to chew trees using our teeth."

Fluffy recalled that since day one of his birth, he was told that those rules were engraved using their ancestors' nails. He felt perplexed about what is the actual truth. Grandy continued, "One fine day, it was raining heavily, and a group of cruel humans came to Greenshire; they grabbed Honky, caged him, and took him along.

They had no idea that I had entered their bag pack. Honky was extremely scared until the night when I revealed myself to Honky. They provided him with food and water but kept him caged. Honky used to save up little food for me, which I enjoyed every night. (Grandy

raises his tone with rage) I knew how to keep friendship, so I came to save him. But he deceived me. We both used to have the same feeling of fear; we both wanted to go back. We used to miss Greenshire and its trees, shrubs, and herbs. Life was miserable, but the bond of friendship was still blooming. And (Grandy's throat gets sore as he talks) the day came when they took Honky somewhere away from me. I kept on searching for him for days and nights. I had no food to eat. Those were tough days of my life; thankfully, I was young and muscular. I travelled so much. I started learning the ways of human life. What do they like, and what do they dislike? You know, my boy, Experience is the best teacher. Life taught me several lessons."

Till now, Fluffy was listening patiently, but now he interrupted and asked, "Did you ever find Honky? If you were such good friends then, why do you hate him now?"

Grandy once again took a deep breath and said, "Well! All are not like me. I never knew that Honky would change this much. He refused to recognize me when I met him in the market after searching for him so much, exactly after 6 months, 24 days, 36 minutes, and 48 seconds." Fluffy got stunned, "What? He didn't recognize you, but you were both good friends."

Grandy got emotional and cried, "He was changed. My friend was changed. His hair was groomed. His teeth were cleaned. He became rich, and he had a human friend. He made new friends. He danced with them. He brought the ball for him whenever his human friend threw it somewhere. He moved around his human friend in circles. He licked him. I heard one of the humans' telling others that he had a pet. Humans even changed his name. They called him 'Tommy.'

I was nowhere. He never turned to see me. How was I doing? Nothing, He didn't even come to check on me. I left Greenshire and came here, and he left me for humans."

After hearing the sad story of Grandy, Fluffy sort of hates his clan. He had always been proud of being Honky, and today all his pride was shattered. He was already in great trouble, and listening to Grandy's story and how his dead grandfather deceived the old kind rat had multiplied his sadness.

It was the time when he recalled yet another rule,

"Whether the story is pathetic or interesting
 Or the Earth felt like deceiving,
 Honkies believe in investigating."

Though Fluffy was chained, he had got some inner strength. His soul still inclined to his clan, and he believed that his dead grandfather would never do this to any of his friends. He now wanted to investigate this matter. But how?

He got a grip on all his emotions and told Grandy politely, "Grandy, did Honky ever tell you that he disliked you or he doesn't know you?"

Grandy thought a bit, paused, and said, "Not really, but then he never came to me." Fluffy replied, "Grandy! Are you living in the same house where you met last?"

Grandy got angry, "I think the story was too sad for you, my boy, so you have lost your mind. How could a rat like me spend a whole life in the same house? We keep on changing places in search of food." Fluffy replied abruptly, "That's the point, Grandy. How do you know if ever Honky had returned to see you, you were not even at that place?"

Grandy sighed, "Oh my innocent boy, even if I was not here, I have a lot of children to tell my whereabouts. Honky was a traitor, and he deceived me. He never deserved my friendship", he added.

31st May 2022, it's been a month and ten days since Fluffy had stepped outside the Greenshire and lost himself.

Grandy and Fluffy had become good companions. Young Fluffy was learning different lessons each day by hearing other stories from Grandy, who only appeared during the night, shared the food provided to Fluffy, and talked to him.

Back there in Greenshire, the whole Honky clan was worried about Fluffy. His parents were trying to trace him through his smell. Fluffy's mother wanted Fluffy back at any cost and was ready to sacrifice anything for it. Till now, they have got an idea that Fluffy was with Humans, and they must have chained him.

But they had yet to learn that humans have brought Fluffy deep inside the crowded areas of the city. It was a pet shop. They kept Fluffy aloof, hidden in a basement area because Fluffy belongs to a scarce and expensive dog species, and selling such rare species was banned by law. And the pet shop owner was waiting for the right customer to come and buy him a high prize.

Fluffy's parents were scared to come to a crowded city as they were aware of Human nature and that their species was one of the richest and rarest, which every human wants as a pet. As we know, mother nature has her plans, and she has chosen Fluffy this time. Seeing a butterfly in the basement was so rare, but he did. It was 28, November, 2022 when Fluffy saw a butterfly once again. It was a beautiful butterfly with blue and green color wings.

The butterfly circled the Janitor lady's human hair with a flower decoration. Fluffy saw that butterfly and was unable to resist it.

He pushed very hard, unknowingly several times, and finally, the chain broke, and he ran after the butterfly. The janitor lady sat on a monster, and so did the Fluffy. Nobody noticed him doing so. The Monster was rolling speedily on the black slide. The butterfly disappeared mysteriously again, making Fluffy realize that he had again put himself into a bigger problem by chasing that tiny silly butterfly.

He was angry with himself and regretted the day he had first seen a butterfly and loved her wings and got this weird habit of chasing butterflies. Suddenly, he heard Grandy's voice pleading for help. "Help! Help! I am drowning." Grandy shouted. Fluffy, unable to figure out where precisely the voice was coming from, asked, "Where are you, Grandy? Where are you?"

Grandy screamed, "I am in this fake lake just before you. Humans called it bucket."

Fluffy moved a step forward and looked inside the giant red bucket. Grandy was struggling for life.

Fluffy quickly bends his neck inside; Grandy jumps a little, holds Fluffy's nose, and comes out of the bucket. Grandy was wet and shivering.

"It is winter, and the sun is about to set. To be alive, you need some warmth. But how did you end up drowning in the bucket, Grandy?" Fluffy questioned.

"When you were blindly running to chase that silly butterfly, you bumped into the pole where I was standing to nibble my food, blew me up, and I fell in the water bucket, drowning myself nearly to death; thankfully, you heard me crying and saved me." Replied Grandy in a shivering voice. Grandy was in utter need of warmth; his body was wet and extremely cold. Fluffy invited Grandy to come and sit under his tail to get little warmth, and Grandy did so, and soon he felt better.

The Monster stopped, and Fluffy cried, "Now what, Grandy? The Monster has stopped moving." Grandy got frightened and ran out from the place he was crouching himself. "Where on the Earth is Monster? I had never seen Monster in my whole life. Where is it?"

Fluffy giggled, "We are traveling on the Monster, and you are asking me where is the Monster?" Grandy pointed to the carrier of the pickup truck and said, "Are you calling this Monster?"

Fluffy said, "Yes! of course, what else could be Monster? It has two sun-like eyes, and its Fart is disgustingly suffocating.

It changed the color of my fur to brown,

and I felt sick. Its BROOM BROOM sound is so horrible. Look at the speed they are rolling on black slides." Grandy started laughing hysterically.

Fluffy added, "At first, I was terrified to sit on it, but now I enjoy riding on it."

Grandy was still laughing and then said, "My innocent boy! These are not Monsters. These are vehicles made by Humans.

God has bestowed humans with mighty minds, and through their intelligence, they have invented many new things which make their life more comfortable and enjoyable."

Fluffy asked curiously, "So what is it called then?" Grandy replied, "This is called CAR; the two suns are light that removes darkness using energy, and that Fart is dirty smoke causing pollution worldwide."

"These Humans are the most selfish species God has created; they only think of their benefits and comfort. They kept on inventing new things which are good for them but extremely harmful to the environment, but this never bothered them.

They never think about us." He added.
One old voice interrupted, "That's not the complete truth. All humans are not bad. Few of them think about us too. They have discovered and invented new medicines to treat us using their brilliant mind and even taking good care of their pets. They are loyal friends, and they are emotional too."
Fluffy and Grandy together asked, "Who is that?" A healthy but old shabby Furry Fluffy Dog showed up.
Grandy was stunned, and Fluffy asked, "Who are you, Sir?"
Grandy shouted, "You traitor, You cheat; you are still alive. I heard you are dead."
Fluffy questioned once again, "Who are you, Sir?" Grandy answered, "He is the one who deceived me.
The one whose story I told you. He is HONKY."
Fluffy was happy, surprised, and confused altogether.
He was happy to find out that his grandfather was alive and was standing

happily in front of him, surprised to find him in these circumstances and confused about how to react. Fluffy always follows his heart. He quickly ran and hugged his grandfather, telling him that he was Fluffy, his grandson. Honky caressed him and licked him everywhere to show his love. Grandy was shocked to know that Fluffy also belonged to Honky clan; he shouted, "Deceiving is in your blood. You liar! You never told me that you are Honky too. I, too, never recognized you due to your brown fur."

Honky spoke clearly, "I am still your old friend 'Honky'. I never changed Mike (Grandy's real name). I was distancing myself from you."

"Oh, really Honky! And why on Earth were you doing so?" questioned Grandy in a raged tone.

Honky answered politely, "Because I don't want you to be in trouble. I was trying to save you." "Save me! Save me from what?" screamed Grandy.

"The day you met me in the market, exactly after 6 months, 24 days, 36 minutes, and 48 seconds of our separation, I was forced to become a trained pet of a very cruel Human who was a mad scientist like other humans called him.

He was searching for rats to do silly experiments on them. I deliberately didn't listen to you so that you would get hurt and never come to see me again. I was scared for your life." Honky replied.

"But a few days back, he died accidentally in an experiment. He had no children or wife or relative. So, I became the owner of his grand house and all his belongings by law.

The carriage car in which you are standing belongs to me now.

The janitor lady driving this carriage car also worked for a scientist. She is a kind lady human. All humans are not cruel. She is a friend of mine." He added.

Grandy's heart got melted, and he started crying. Honky moved forward and gave him a tight hug. Both the friends got united.

Fluffy was watching and listening to everything quietly. Honky invited Fluffy to come, and the three of them had a group hug. Fluffy got contended that now he would reach home safely and happily.

So, this was the plan of mother nature to reunite the old friends and test the most eligible Honky of Greenshire.

But one question still lingers on Fluffy's mind, "Why on Earth was he told that Honkies used their ancestors; nails for engraving rules on the Banyan tree, but Grandy said to him that he did it himself using his teeth?"

So, he asked the same of Grandy and Honky. Grandy and Honky laughed loudly and replied, "That's another long story young boy; we will tell you way back to Greenshire."

Fluffy, Grandy, and Honky started their journey back to Greenshire on the same carriage. Fluffy told Honky about all the other grandchildren he had. All about Zinker, Zonky, and Mala, and he was missing all of them.

Glossary

DID I GET THE BEST?

Fondness - affection or liking for someone or something.

Gossiping - engage in gossip.

Terrified - cause to feel extreme fear

Engulfed - eat or swallow (something) whole

Unique - being the only one of its kind; unlike anything else

Triggered - (of a response) caused by particular action, process, or situation.

Reluctantly - in an unwilling and hesitant way.

Tripping - walk, run, or dance with quick light steps.

Fidgeting - be impatient or uneasy

Allergic - of, relating to, affected with, or caused by allergy. an allergic reaction: having a dislike for something

Murmured - say something in a low or indistinct voice.

Ferocious - very great; extreme

Robust - strong and healthy; vigorous

Fluffy of Greenshire

Engraved – cut or carve (a text or design) on the surface of a hard object.

Ancestors - a person, typically one more remote than a grandparent, from whom one is descended.

Mesmerize - capture the complete attention of (someone)

Mysteriously - in a way that is difficult or impossible to understand, explain, or identify.

Vibrantly - in a way that is full of life and energy

Suffocating - causing difficulty in breathing.

Heebity – Jeebities - a condition of extreme nervousness caused by fear, worry, strain, etc.; the jitters; the willies

Exhausted - very tired.

Accomplished – finished

Screeching - (of a person or animal) give a loud, harsh, piercing cry.

Horrifying - causing horror; extremely shocking.

Annoying- causing irritation or annoyance

Pathetic - arousing pity, especially through vulnerability or sadness

Civilized - at an advanced stage of social and cultural development

Revealing - making interesting or significant information known, especially of a personal nature

Lingering - lasting for a long time or slow to end

Distracted - unable to concentrate because one is preoccupied by something worrying or unpleasant.

Stubborn - having or showing dogged determination not to change one's attitude or position on something, especially in spite of good arguments or reasons to do so.

Deceived - deliberately cause (someone) to believe something that is not true, especially for personal gain.
Miserable - (of a person) wretchedly unhappy or uncomfortable.
Interrupted - stop the continuous progress of (an activity or process)
Recognize - identify (someone or something) from having encountered them before; know again.
Groomed - having a clean and neat appearance that is produced with care
Shattered - break or cause to break suddenly and violently into pieces
Investigate - carry out a systematic or formal inquiry to discover and examine the facts of (an incident, allegation, etc.) so as to establish the truth.
Abruptly - suddenly and unexpectedly
Perplexed - completely baffled; very puzzled.
Deserved - rightfully earned because of something done or qualities shown
Species - a kind or sort
Regretted - feel sad, repentant, or disappointed over (something that one has done or failed to do).
Nibble - take small bites out of.
Frightened - afraid or anxious.
Crouching - adopt a position where the knees are bent and the upper body is brought forward and down, typically in order to avoid detection or to defend oneself.
Giggled – laugh lightly and repeatedly in a silly way, from amusement, nervousness, or embarrassment.

Hysterically - in an extremely excited way and without any control, often with crying or laughter

Bestowed - confer or present (an honor, right, or gift).

Pollution - the presence in or introduction into the environment of a substance which has harmful or poisonous effects.

Caressed - touch or stroke gently or lovingly.

Contended - struggle to surmount (a difficulty)

www.ingramcontent.com/pod-product-compliance
Lightning Source LLC
LaVergne TN
LVHW020416070526
838199LV00054B/3634